Facts About the Quokka

By Lisa Strattin

© 2016 Lisa Strattin

Facts for Kids Picture Books by Lisa Strattin

Pygmy Possum, Vol 143

Pygmy Goat, Vol 144

Pygmy Hippo, Vol 145

Pygmy Falcon, Vol 146

Pygmy Marmoset, Vol 147

Pygmy Elephant, Vol 148

Pygmy Owl, Vol 149

Carpet Python, Vol 150

Ball Python, Vol 151

Eastern Diamondback Rattlesnake, Vol 152

Sign Up for New Release Emails Here

http://lisastrattin.com/subscribe-here

Join the KidCrafts Monthly Program Here

http://KidCraftsByLisa.com

All rights reserved. No part of this book may be reproduced by any means whatsoever without the written permission from the author, except brief portions quoted for purpose of review.

All information in this book has been carefully researched and checked for factual accuracy. However, the author and publisher makes no warranty, express or implied, that the information contained herein is appropriate for every individual, situation or purpose and assume no responsibility for errors or omissions. The reader assumes the risk and full responsibility for all actions, and the author will not be held responsible for any loss or damage, whether consequential, incidental, special or otherwise, that may result from the information presented in this book.

I have relied on my own observations as well as many different sources for this book and I have done my best to check facts and give credit where it is due. In the event that any material is used without proper permission, please contact me so that the oversight can be corrected.

Table of Contents

INTRODUCTION 6
CHARACTERISTICS 8
APPEARANCE 10
LIFE STAGES 12
LIFE SPAN 14
SIZE 16
HABITAT 18
DIET 20
FRIENDS AND ENEMIES 22
SUITABILITY AS PETS 24
PLUSH QUOKKA 37
KIDCRAFTS MONTHLY SUBSCRIPTION PROGRAM 38

INTRODUCTION

The quokka is a type of marsupial found on the continent of Australia. Although they vary in size from the large kangaroo to this small quokka, they all have large feet with powerful legs and tails. The quokka is currently labeled as vulnerable by the International Union for Conservation of Nature. This is mostly due to human interference such as logging and introducing new species to its native habitats.

CHARACTERISTICS

The quokka seems to smile, so it has been called "the happiest animal in the world." This has made the animal very popular to take selfies with on Rottnest Island. They seem to have no fear of humans and will get really close. However, it is illegal to touch or feed the animals and you could be fined. The quokka are herbivores and nocturnal for the most part. From far away the quokka may look like a small cat or large rat. They appear to be hunched over with its tail behind it

APPEARANCE

The quokka's body is rounded. It has both short ears and a short tail. The fur is short and a brownish color. It has small, dark eyes and a small mouth with a larger nose. Its face narrows making it appear to smile. When first seen explorer Willem de Vlamingh thought they were rats and named the island "rat's nest" in Dutch, or Rottnest. These animals are cute and cuddly. But, they also have sharp claws and teeth. So, be careful. They stand on their hind legs often holding up their smaller front legs, similar to the kangaroo and wallaby. Their feet are darker in color and slender and long.

LIFE STAGES

Like a kangaroo, babies are called "joeys" and are born after just one month in the mother's womb. However, it will stay in its mother's pouch for another six months before venturing out into the world. It will continue to nurse, or drink its mother's milk, for another couple of months. It will be ready to become a parent itself in only one and half years. They usually raise only one joey a year.

LIFE SPAN

Quokkas live an average of ten years. Most of its predators have been introduced to the area by humans and are not natural predators; such as the fox and other domesticated pets, cats and dogs, specifically. Clearing of its habitat for logging and destruction of vegetation from tourists also contribute to its decline in population.

SIZE

The quokka weighs between five and ten pounds, it stands about ten inches tall and between sixteen and twenty-one inches long. Its tail may be an additional foot long.

HABITAT

Like other marsupials, it calls Australia home. It can be found in the far southwestern corner and coastal islands of Australia. Rottnest Island is famous for them, being named after them. Only smaller colonies can be found on the mainland today, in a reserve. Quokkas like to live in communities of twenty-five to one hundred and fifty. These colonies are protected by the dominant males of the group. These colonies can be found close to water sources usually in tall grasses. The quokka like swamplands which make them easy targets for snakes.

DIET

The quokka is an herbivore, eating only plants. It eats a variety of leaves and grasses. It may climb trees to look for food. However, its favorite food is a flowering plant. It also enjoys succulents, which are plants that have fat, fleshy areas that hold water and are juicy. They prefer to look for food at night. They are capable of going without food or water for long periods though. During this time, they can survive off of the fat that has been stored in their tails. Quokkas do not chew their food, but rather swallow it whole. They then chew the cud- like a cow. This allows the quokka to absorb more nutrients from the food.

FRIENDS AND ENEMIES

The fox is the most feared predator of the quokka. There are no foxes on the islands it inhabits making it a safe zone for the quokka. On the island of Rottnest, the snake is its only predator. But, on the mainland, it is a different story. The quokka must hide in dense cover to survive on the mainland. This is why it considered a "vulnerable" species. Another danger is that visitors to the island feed the quokka human food, which may cause the animal to become very ill

SUITABILITY AS PETS

Since the quokka is nocturnal, keeping one as a pet, playing with it during the day would disrupt its natural behavior and activities. Also, remember they have sharp claws and teeth. So, you could get hurt from these smiling creatures It would also need to be protected and kept safe from other household pets. Also, the production of commercial food is not readily available and it may become difficult to provide it with enough of its natural favorites continually. Thus, the quokka would not make the best family pet.

Please leave me a review here:

http://lisastrattin.com/Review-Vol-158

For more Kindle Downloads Visit Lisa Strattin Author Page on Amazon Author Central

http://amazon.com/author/lisastrattin

To see upcoming titles, visit my website at LisaStrattin.com – all books available on kindle!

http://lisastrattin.com

PLUSH QUOKKA

You can get one by copying and pasting this link into your browser:

http://lisastrattin.com/QuokkaPlush

KIDCRAFTS MONTHLY SUBSCRIPTION PROGRAM

Receive a Box of Crafts and a Lisa Strattin Full Color Paperback Book Each Month in Your Mailbox!

Get yours by copying and pasting this link into your browser

http://KidCraftsByLisa.com

Printed in Poland
by Amazon Fulfillment
Poland Sp. z o.o., Wrocław